MINDFUL
FLATULENCE

MINDFUL
FLATULENCE

Focus, De-stress and
Find Your Release

Gus T. Blooms

Michael O'Mara Books Limited

First published in Great Britain in 2020 by
Michael O'Mara Books Limited
9 Lion Yard
Tremadoc Road
London SW4 7NQ

A CIP catalogue record for this book is available
from the British Library.

Papers used by Michael O'Mara Books Limited are natural, recyclable
products made from wood grown in sustainable forests. The
manufacturing processes conform to the environmental regulations of
the country of origin.

ISBN: 978-1- 78929-313-5 in paperback print format
ISBN: 978-1-78929-314-2 in ebook format

1 2 3 4 5 6 7 8 9 10

Printed and bound by CPI Group (UK) Ltd, Croydon, CR0 4YY

www.mombooks.com

CONTENTS

INTRODUCING MINDFUL FLATULENCE

May the blessings of many gentle zephyrs be within you. And good evening, if you are reading this in the evening. I would like to begin by telling you how I chose the path I have taken. It is a spiritual path, a rewarding path, a windy path. I was born Gustav Tony Blooms Junior. The 'Junior' because my father was also a Gustav and the Blooms because that was our surname. You work it out.

I was a child of divorce who lived with my scrupulously clean mother and two sisters, Karen and Bobby. We would visit my father (a historian) every other weekend. On his ninetieth birthday, my father shared with me something wondrous from his attic. It was a tome documenting the history of flatulence in great detail, entitled *The History of Farting*. I was amazed to learn that, for many generations, the Blooms had been the curators of bottom wind lore. My great-great-grandfather passed wind to my grandfather who passed wind to my father who got divorced then passed wind to me.

With this precious tome in my hands, I did what any hippie would do. I put the book down and went off

camping with my best friend 'Quiet Paul', who had just lost his job as an aerobics instructor.

That night, as we gazed up at the stars, our tents pitched, a simple meal of meat and cheese in our bellies, Quiet Paul drifted off to sleep. It was then that his bottom spoke to me. In a night emission booming and loud of which Quiet Paul was completely unaware, I heard these two words:

'GO WELL!' (With the last part of 'well' tapering up high.)

I knew then that it was my duty to take our family history of flatulence to the next level and to use it as a path towards mindfulness, wellbeing and enlightenment.

The next morning, I bought a kaftan and became a Gas Cleric, a Father of the Flatulence, or a Puff Daddy if that's nicer. Since then, I have been reaching inward to give off everything I can to those who follow my church – the church of flatulent mindfulness. The tome you hold now contains all the knowledge I've cooked up since that day.

I deal it to you now. Go well.

Most exonerated Gus T. Blooms
Gust Guru and Spiritual Guide

THE TOWN FART AND THE COUNTRY FART: A FARTING FABLE

A town fart and a country fart were best friends and they were also farts. One day, they decided to visit each other. The Town Fart came to the country first to see the Country Fart's home. The Town Fart was disappointed at the Country Fart's standard of humble living. As a fart, all you could do there was emerge from a cow or maybe a farmer's bottom. The Town Fart did not enjoy passing unnoticed in the rural air.

'You must visit me in the town. There are many people's bottoms to escape out of and it can be really exhilarating. It is a melting pot there,' said the Town Fart.

So the Country Fart visited the Town Fart and enjoyed escaping from the bottoms of bankers and judges and librarians but soon pined for the freedom of the country and the spiritual peace of coming out of a cow's back.

The two farts realized that what was right for one fart was not right for another and, after a big hug, decided to appreciate each other's 'cultures' and keep visiting each other.

The moral of the story is thus: we have more in common than that which divides us (and one of the things we have in common is flatulence which, ironically, often divides us).

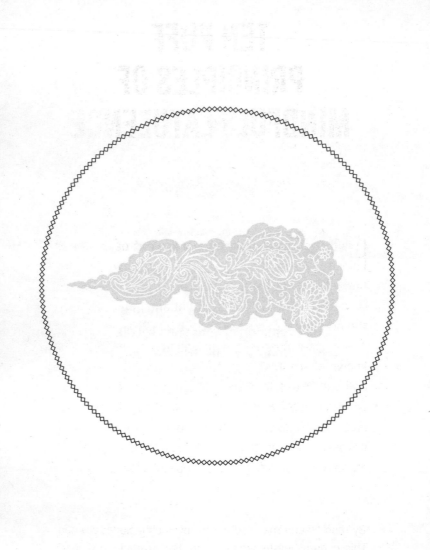

TEN PUFF PRINCIPLES OF MINDFUL FLATULENCE

I t is thought that back vapoury law has been around since the first sentient man* became aware of his first eructation. From that time, humans have been on a passageway to betterment and peace through the noise and gas of their back passageways.

A great charter of flatulent freedoms, otherwise known as the 'Magna Farta', was recorded in AD 1215 and within this tome are written ten basic principles which all acolytes of the windy way must follow. As a reader of this book, you too are now such an acolyte, so it is essential to grasp these following ten principles. Gas mastery is at your fingertips, if you just allow it . . .

*By 'man' I mean 'mankind' which obviously includes women. This cannot be stressed enough. For example, my sister Bobby produces enough wind on a daily basis to power an industrial lathe.

1

To hold that each flatulence is unique.

2

**To hold that each flatulence
provides us with insight.**

3

**To hold that flatulence can
and will occur at any time.**

4

To not hold off any flatulence.

5

To be in tune at all times with one's own flatulence.

6

That a flatulence is a bottom air and not an air from any other part of the body.

7

**That no flatulantee is superior
to any other flatulentee.**

8

**That all flatulentees must
encourage other flatulentees
to be flatulently mindful.**

9

**That all flatulentees both indoors
and outdoors are free.**

10

**That 'flatulantee'
is an actual word.**

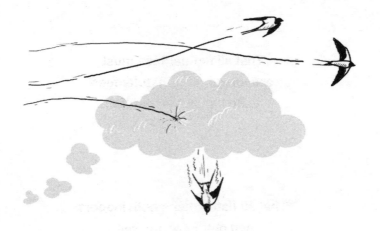

TEN BASIC MINDFUL FLATULENT YOGIC POSITIONS

Wind contrology is something practised by all schools of mindful flatulence. It is well known that many Wind Ministers, Blast Clerks, Waft Deacons, Blow Abbots and Parp Diocesans take different approaches to mindful flatulence. For example, the Blast Clerks of Scandinavia follow every eructation with a high kick and the loud declaration, 'Kom på mig nu uheld! For jeg er skjult af selvtågen.'*

Yet all schools agree on the basic stances and positions. These simple positions are listed here. With a little practice, they will no doubt come as naturally as the air itself that wisps from our backs on a daily basis.

*'Come at me now misfortune! I am shielded by the fog of self!'

THE BIG-EYED CROW

PASSAGASATA

This common position can be used for the simplest of exercises. It is common because it is widely used and is called the Big-eyed Crow because the position involves the eyes going big like those of a crow, say. A crow with big eyes.

Standing, lean the torso
inwards slightly and brace.

Widen the eyes with bewilderment,
like one is listening to the radio in the
1940s (uncertain of the news).

Be careful not to bulge the eyes whilst
forcing any gas. Quiet Paul did that
once and got a detached retina.

THE TROUBLED PANTHER

PUMPAWTBAWKWARDA

This is a position suitable for long-awaited or deeply welcomed flatulence for the times we experience discomfort and strife. The position addresses and contends with the personal security we all feel within ourselves day to day. To this end, it is perfect that the position is named after the panther. The panther is one of the most overlooked of all of the big cats,* receiving good PR only in Rudyard Kipling's *The Jungle Book* and nowhere else of note.

Gently get onto all fours with elbows flat on
the ground with lower legs flat onto the floor.

Arch the back.

Create a gentle rocking motion, like any of
the big cats about to sprint for quarry.

*The lynx was previously the least popular of the big cats
until the relatively recent introduction of the body spray of
the same name. Interestingly, this body spray is rumoured
to contain flatulence.

THE SHATTERED PUFFIN

FLATBAKAFLATULAWA

This more advanced position is best used for severe situations or the most ambitious of flatulent meditation. The position could have been named after any bird that must contend with exhaustion. It is named 'the shattered puffin', however, because a puffin all tired and breathy after funnelling fish down itself all day is easier to visualize than a snow petrel doing the same.

Lie firmly on your back on a bed or the floor.

Bring the legs upward to the chest.

Move the legs upwards and downwards slowly
to encourage the flow of your back gas.

Keep your arms at your side at all times
and imagine they are shorter, like the
wings of a puffin or snow petrel.

THE DOWNWARD BOAR

COPYCATAWATA

Much like the downward dog, except boar instead of dog, this position can give a sense of togetherness, levity and originality. It is a steadying position that will supply us with inner determination, like that of the dog or boar.

Stand on a non-slippy surface
in shoes that will not slip.

Assume the yogic downward dog position
by placing your hands on the floor and
lifting your rear to the ceiling, setting it free.
Now tuck the toes and lift the hips. Let the
neck be long with the rest of the spine.

Constantly refer to the
Downward Boar position.*

*In the same way that new practitioners of yoga never stop
mentioning the 'Downward Dog' to anyone and everyone, so
to must you, as a newly mindful flatulentee not cease from
dropping 'Downward Boar' into every conversation.

THE FLYING STARFISH

FLAPAWALA-UPAFARFAR

This is an ambitious position in that it requires the flatulantee to become briefly airborne whilst dispensing of bottom miasma. Important: do not try this if you are not able bodied, have a fear of very low heights or have low ceilings.

In firm gripping pumps,*
stand on a flat surface with
arms by the sides.

❁

Wait for the press of release of your
miasma and, as you feel it, leap upwards
into the air, extending your arms and
legs like Leonardo da Vinci's Vitruvian
Man, but Vitruvian Man in the air.

❁

*By 'firm gripping pumps', I mean of course sneakers
and not lingering flatulence. Although there have been
cases of firm gripping pumps in this latter sense.
Either Quiet Paul or I dispensed gas in a yurt once and
it stayed for so long that we forgot what life was like
before it.

Gasses may be released once
one is in the air. As you begin to descend,
bring the legs and arms together.

Repeat if you have any more urgent
back air. This position takes some practice
but can be very rewarding. If the timing of
the flatulence is right, one can be propelled
ever so slightly further up into the air.

THE HEATED BULL

MATADAWA-SHATALALA

This is a position originating from the Flatulantadors of Spain but popularized by Fart Deacon Hans Kweb in the late seventeenth century. This is known as one of the HOT flatulent yogic positions. Hot Fart Yoga is associated with anger or urgency, much as the bull can be in other areas of life, and often has crossover with normal yoga as a quick release sometimes just can't be helped.

With head bowed, scrape the
ankles backward one at a time,
as if you are a furious bull boxed
into the trap of a bull ring.

You should now be feeling hot,
angry emotions whilst you are
also helping to propel gasses
downwards and out of you.

THE LISTING MONK (PROUD)

FRIARPARPA (BEAMAHAHA)

This is perhaps the flatulent yogic position that comes the most naturally to humans. Like the monk, it is merry but also deeply focused and determined. It is named after the monk because of the discipline and determination a life of ascetism requires and also because monks eat a lot of bread and cheese.

In seated position, tilt the upper
body to the right or left, depending
on your political leanings.

Continue this until one buttock
is now off the chair.

In this position, blessed gas should be
delivered freely, loudly and with deliberation.

Anyone present will be either dismayed
or entertained at the theatricality of it.

For best results and optimum noise, ensure
you are seated on a leather chair.

THE LISTING MONK
(BASHFUL)

FRIARPARPA (GROWDSWALLAWA)

This is another instinctive position. It is very similar to the Listing Monk (Proud) but relies on much less distinct or deliberate movements. The essence of this pose is in how you use the pressure of the gas to make a quiet yet prolonged release, making this both an enjoyable yet progressively surprising noise for your companion.

In a seated position, pull
a deeply bashful face.

✸

Tilt the upper body to the right or left
depending who is in the vicinity. If
there is someone to your left, then you
should tilt right and vice versa.

✸

Gas should be released with one
buttock raised with a sorrowful
expression on the face.

✸

A profuse apology should follow when
releasing in Listing Monk (Bashful).

THE BAD OWL

NAWTINAWCTUNRA

This is a passive or stealth position for mindful flatulence. More experienced flatulentees can attempt this exercise alongside a 180-degree turn of the head but please do note that this requires sufficient warming up of the neck and the buttocks to avoid injury.

Centre your body such that it is still.

Tighten the buttocks, mindfully guarding
the gateway here to the outside world.

Ensure your eyes are wide open and feel
the movement of the eyes only.

Releases of miasma should occur without
moving the body at all, moving only the eyes.

Note: Quiet Paul experienced the ire of a real bad
owl once, although this one was not passive like
the position here. It had simply not detected Quiet
Paul as he walked up a country path due to Paul's
stealthy gait and flew fully into his face. As feathers

shot everywhere Quiet Paul shouted, 'There's an owl on my face . . . Help! An owl is on my face. Not the eyes, not the eyes!' but was unable to alert any nearby ramblers as Quiet Paul shouting is the equivalent of an asthmatic librarian whispering.

THE COGENT SEA LION

SLOBALAWA-PASSALARJWAN

This is the most extreme position of all the mindfully flatulent poses. It can be used in medical emergencies where extreme trapped air is causing difficulty. For this reason, it is often good to have a birthing partner present.

With knees flat on the floor, adopt a semi prone position. If you are attempting the Cogent Sea

Lion alone, hands can be turned outward,
flat on the ground, like you are someone who
can't do press ups trying to do a press up.

If you are with a birthing partner, it is wise to
have them hold your hands with theirs such
that they can rock you back and forth.

If you have a partner, do this and have them
rock you back and forth. If you do not, use
the ground to rock yourself back and forth.

You will at this point want to wail low like a sea lion.

Regardless of whether you are with
partner or not repeat the mantra, 'This is
it . . . here it comes . . . this is the one.'

THE WIND, THE SUN AND THE MAN: A FARTING FABLE

Once there was a weary beta cis male who toiled day and night making shoes for children and the blind. The man was well mannered and hard-working and loved by all, including the Wind and the Sun up in the Heavens.

It was time for the man to take his well-earned holiday. The Wind and the Sun watched him lay alone on the crowded beach next to a party of nuns, who had travelled from the countryside.

The Sun turned to the Wind and said, 'Let's see which of us is the most powerful; the one to cause the man to leave the beach is the winner.' They agreed.

The Sun went first. He beamed his rays hard onto the man, making him sweat, but this just caused the man to smile and take his top off and some of the nuns to take their wimples off. The more the sun beamed onto the man, the more the man relaxed and bathed.

It was now the turn of the clever Wind. The Wind was as quick as a flash and flew down from the Heavens and into the man, causing the man to do the biggest involuntary fart that anyone has ever done. Unable to look the nuns in the eye, the man raced away from the beach, red-faced with shame and sunburn, but mostly from shame from the loud fart.

The moral of the story is thus:
one second of focus is more
valuable than hours of idleness.

MINDFUL FLATULENCE EXERCISES

It is important to remember that all followers of the windy way 'practise' mindful flatulence. Many people consider flatulence to be an exercise within itself. Indeed, flatulence can be the only exercise that some people get.

The exercises listed here, however, have been practised and refined for many years and all are considered to be deeply fulfilling. Some are more advanced than others so it is important to go at your own pace. It is also important to forgive yourself on days when you do not practise or when your wind has totally gone out of control, causing you to lose concentration and fall into your best friend's glass coffee table, rendering it 'completely irreparable'.* Go well.

* I am happy to report that Quiet Paul has now fully paid for the replacement of my glass coffee table over a period of monthly instalments.

THE EFFLUVIUM SCAN

This welcoming exercise has been performed by Wind Trappist monks in Tibet for centuries in order to relieve discomfort from bloating or any kind of spiritual gas blockage. It is perfect for anyone beset by worry, trapped wind, or anyone worried about trapped wind.

The exercise is designed to turn your attention to the various parts of your body that are withholding air and comes in two parts.

To start, lie in a comfortable position on your back with head back and stomach protruding (like a cartoon mouse on a Christmas card that's eaten a huge dinner).

Now bring your attention to your gut, scanning in your mind from the top to the bottom and focusing with calm acceptance as to where the wind may be.

Once you have pinpointed a pocket of air, try to imagine it as a docile donkey, moving slowly down a winding mountain, peaceably and with no rush or sense of alarm.

While this is happening, you may want to continue the Effluvium Scan and trust that donkey will get to the bottom of the mountain and out into the fresh forest of relief.

Any other pockets of air you find, think of them
too like a donkey. But not the same donkey.
This is a different donkey, with a different
personality and a different name, if need be.

Breathe and remain calm as all of
your donkeys move to the bottom of
the imagined mountain (your gut).

As one reaches the bottom, so should it be
released. Imagine the donkey has developed
wings and is flying up into the heavens.
Think of how high it has floated. Where
is it now? And now? And now?

⊛

As your mind wanders, you may turn your
attention back to the other donkeys still
making their way down the mountain path.

⊛

Continue, until your mountain path is donkey free.
Notice your relaxed state and carry it
with you for the rest of your day.

THE SELF APPRAISAL

Flatulence can mean many things and take many forms. Yet most importantly it is as a vital reminder to be calm about who we are. This easy exercise can be carried out anywhere you experience flatulence. At home, on the way to work, at work or, if you're anything like me, every time you step into a public library.

 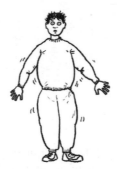 

Wearing loose fitting clothing,* proceed
lightly with your daily routine, until you
feel the sudden inward call of nature.

At the moment you feel this, close your
eyes (unless you are driving) and exhale.
Release your internal miasma.

*Loose fitting clothing is something embraced by all
members of the church of flatulence. This is because
it can be easily wafted to create an urgent makeshift
fan. Advocates of the windy way don these garbs out
of politeness and respect to others. Also, and entirely
separately, there is little in the world more liberating than
going for a pee in a kaftan.

Inhale the miasma, noting what you sense
from the miasma. In this moment, be aware
that you are 'reading yourself'.

The cloud may be awful or it may be
odourless. Yet you will always accept it.
Flatulence is a reminder of self-acceptance.
It is a miracle that such a foul cloud can
be tolerated by yourself or at
times even enjoyed.

Say very loudly, 'This is me. And I
accept myself in the world.'
Then, continuing to wear loosely fitted
clothing, go about your day.

HARVESTING REGRET

There are times when our flatulence can feel destructive and unbearable. In these moments, it is worth focusing on wrong decisions or what might have been. This simple exercise offers an opportunity to reflect on such moments.

Ensure that you are alone at home and that you don't expect your spouse or children back for the next three hours. Our negative miasmas hang together in the same way that depressed drunks at bars often do. Misery loves company.

Straddle a chair or, if you don't have
a chair, fashion one from wood.

Wait for the phase of negative miasma and focus
on the last bad decision you made. (This could
be a difficult to digest meal, a row with a partner
or the decision to build a wooden chair.)

When the gas is imminent, imagine the decision
has had deeply reaching consequences. This
could be food poisoning, a trial separation
or splinters that have led to sepsis.

Release the bad gas and remember at
that moment that the bad consequences
were only imagined.

Feel your troubles hang together for a while,
then disperse. Savour your new peace.

PRIMAL COLONIC ROAR

Anger, frustration and determination can build up in us like back wind after a badly washed salad leading to loud reports. Should you sense that the volume of your zephyrs has been turned up to full, then use this opportunity for a Primal Colonic Roar.

Clear your mind almost entirely, leaving
just enough mindset to straddle a chair.

As you feel the surge of gasses burgeon for exit,
channel all of your anger and frustration into
them. Think back to many different times you were
overlooked and were too polite to say anything.

Hold for ten seconds, letting
the anger build in you.

❂

Release the wind angrily while shouting
'I AM A CHILD OF THE UNIVERSE' at a
volume befitting your environment.

❂

Feel that the universe has
acknowledged your statement.
Thank it. Then breathe calmly.

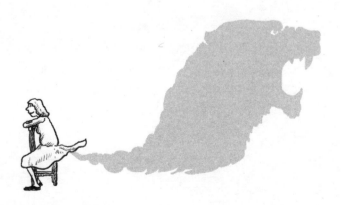

TIP

You should repeat this exercise weekly, otherwise an excess of zephyrs can lead to Harvesting Regret (see page 59).

THE GAS WHISPERER

Most readers will be familiar with the question, 'What does your gut tell you?' For it is here we feel wisdom and guidance. Wind Trappist monks have long believed that the gut is wise and portentous and, if listened to properly, that our gasses carry answers and messages.

Assume the Big-eyed Crow position,
relax your lower body and visualize
yourself stepping up to an ancient
oracle. The oracle of your gut.

If you have a question, then ask it out
loud. This could be 'Should I go to Dave's
tonight?' or 'Can I trust anyone in my book
group?' or any other question that
requires a yes/no response.

Wait patiently for the reply
to arrive in gas form.

A bottom note that starts lower and goes
high can be interpreted as a 'Yes'.

✹

A bottom note descending from high
to low is a resounding 'No'.

✹

A bottom note that wavers up and down
means that your gut has no way of
knowing the answer at this time.

THE LOUD RETREAT

Group flatulence can be a real source of comfort in times of uncertainty. For centuries, the Air Benders of Tibet would gather together in caves to enjoy the union and din of their loudly escaping gas.

Gather a number of family or friends in a
well-aired space after a group meal.

❋

Ensure all digital equipment is turned off.

❋

Close all curtains and blinds.

❋

Set a timer for the length of the retreat.
Three hours is a good starting point.

❋

Form a circle with everyone in
Cogent Sea Lion position.

❋

Repeat as a group: 'In our safe cave
here, our words are for birds and nothing
but our wind shall be heard.'

❋

Everyone is then encouraged to make blessed
wind as loudly as possible for the duration.

❋

Try to accept the effusions of others
as you would your own.
Smiling and laughter is permitted.

THE LONG NOTE

OR 'DIDGERIDOO'

In Tibetan Buddhism, 'ohm' is often placed at the beginning of mantras and dharanis. According to the ancient tome, 'The sound of one hand wafting', this word is stretched out long over time to keep monks mindful of the present. In much the same way, we can do this with the release of a long, slow miasma, which can feel calming and rewarding, as well as infinite.

On feeling that there is gas of some length
inside one's body, lie backwards on a bed or
mattress in the Shattered Puffin position.

Calm your mind. It is important not to
become excited at the prospect of lengthy
gaseous release. This could cause
disappointment and bad alignment.

At the point of release, stay focused on the
moment, imagine that this is a regular release
and that time has slowed down, like in a film.

Focus calmly on the even release.

As the seconds pass, it is easy to become
distracted by pride or become fearful once
the release goes over ten seconds. Pay
these emotions no mind and let them go.

You are now achieving fart nirvana by continuing
the release without trying to keep it going.

The moment you become impressed or
anxious you will close the channel of the
anal chakra and the moment will be gone.

THE VICINITY SCAN

This is a simple exercise designed to lessen anxiety at the onset of flatulence in an environment with any level of footfall where flatulence may be undesirable. This could be a workplace or a place of relaxation, like a museum or spa.

On feeling the need to release in a busy environment, stand with the legs slightly apart and arms behind the back, much like a passively alert policeman. Become aware of who is around you. Are they likely to leave soon? When?

Now direct your attention to entrances and
exits. Could a person suddenly emerge
from here? And if so, how long would it take
them to breach a potential miasma?

Become aware also of what is above or below
you. Could a person arrive from above?
This will be unlikely but possible. There could be
someone up a ladder or about to fall out of a window.

Your body will feel ready to release any gas
now that it has performed this simple and
calming reconnaissance. It will have set
parameters that will avoid embarrassment.

If your reconnaissance mission fails, immediately
take up the Big-Eyed Crow pose and stand
tall. And release. Taking ownership of our
flatulence is the only form of action required.

THE TROUBLED JET

Whilst much of the time our backward air flows regularly and instantly there are times when we may feel beset by many pockets of air, causing us great discomfort and worry. I am immediately reminded of a time when Quiet Paul and I took a ski lift in France and he remained very quiet, even by his standards, for the entire duration of the trip. His expression was that of a man who had remembered he had left the iron on in his home. I became aware he was troubled inwardly by many tiny pockets of trapped air and knew straight away what to do. After completing The Troubled Jet exercise, Quiet Paul's intestines were finally at peace.

In Troubled Panther position, close your eyes
and breathe deeply. Become aware of the
many pockets of stifled air within you.
Imagine yourself you are a passenger plane
speeding towards a destination above the clouds.

⊛

Imagine the trapped air to be wind
turbulence. Feel the anxiety of some of
the nervous passengers within.

⊛

Imagine the pilot now telling those passengers
that the turbulence is nothing to worry
about. Become aware also of the cabin crew
who seem perfectly calm despite being buffered
around while they try to serve duty free.

⊛

Once you are aware the trapped air will
not harm you, you will find it makes its way
out readily and gently in due course.

THE TROJAN HORSE

This is a great exercise for times when we really do need to pass undesirable gases and basically 'get away with' bad flatulence in social situations, such as a party or residents' meeting.

On feeling the urge to be flatulent, smile
calmly as if nothing is urgent.

You must now use an element of deception
to take yourself somewhere private. Feel
the joy of the effectiveness of your 'white
lie' as you head towards guff sanctuary.

Savour the new solitude
you have created.

Imagine your gut is a Trojan horse parked safely
within the city walls of Troy and they have no
idea you have deadly soldiers within you.

Let the deadly soldiers slip out of you
one by one, savouring their foulness.

When the last solider has escaped, wait
a good three minutes before heading
back in, ensuring that none of your
military gasses have followed you.*

---

* If there really is no escape then resorting to distractive
measures such as shouting, 'HELP I'VE JUST BEEN
ROBBED!' or setting off any nearby sprinkler system.

WIND SAUSAGES

This is an exercise of measure and restraint. It teaches us control and temperance through flatulence. In Heated Bull position, imagine yourself working a sausage piping machine in a factory. If you eschew meat, like me and Quiet Paul, you can easily pretend the sausages are vegan.

Each time you release your back
air, imagine you have your foot on
the sausage piping pedal.

Press to release an air sausage
then ease off on the pedal.

Try to do this evenly and regularly so
you are now piping shop-standard,
uniform sausages.

If you over-pipe at any time, take
a moment to be amused at how this
must look in sausage form.

THE FOREST CALL

This is an exercise hailing from feudal Japan learned by the Guff Geishas operating in the area there during that time. It is a lesson from the stealth school of yogic flatulence. Also living through these times was the great Shinto air Shifter 'Akifumi' who proffered the following: 'How do you hide a tree? You build a forest around it.' This is exactly the thinking behind the stealthy forest call.

In either Shattered Puffin position or
Big-eyed Crow, ready your gasses.

❀

As you release, make a loud report. A cough or
exclamation will do. Anything short and loud.

❀

With this noise, you are foresting
your own tree in that the sound of it
should be lost within the melee.

TIP

**It is extremely important to get
the timing of your mouth noise in sync
with the timing of your bottom
noise. Anything other than this
will make you appear crazy.**

THE ABSENT DESPOT

One of the most versatile and celebrated exercises in mindful flatulence, the Absent Despot, reminds us of our free will and our basic human right to be comfortable and at peace. It is best enjoyed on waking.

Make sure you are alone or in the
company of those who do not have
issue with your back pneumatics.

❋

In Cogent Sea Lion or Listing Monk (Proud)
position, become aware of your environment.
Perhaps you are in a bed or a chair? If you're
not in a bed or a chair, that's fine also.

❋

Be mindful of a person you know who would
not approve of your bottom gesticulations.
Perhaps this is a strict teacher or an ex-partner.

❋

At the moment of discharge, really visualize
them in the room and feel the judgemental
tension that awaits your blast.

Then remind yourself that
they are not really there.

Fill your face with a smile as you fill
the room with your vapours, savouring
the absence of fart fascists.

THE DOOR KEEPER

In this exercise, we learn more about responsibility, control and balance. In Downward Boar position, close your eyes and imagine you are the doorman of a Roman baths or perhaps, to be more up to date, the bouncer of a busy nightclub. The nightclub is the area immediately surrounding your body. The build of gasses inside you is a stressed-out queue of patrons awaiting entry. At the club, there is a strict 'one in one out' policy which you must oversee in order to keep your job as a bouncer.

Take a deep breath in and imagine
this is a patron leaving the club.

There is now room in the club
for another patron.

As wind leaves your body, imagine
this is a patron entering the club.

❋

Release your gas in a measured fashion as
you 'Allow a new patron into the club'.

❋

Nod at the gas before it enters the club,
so it knows you have approved it.

❋

Observe a group of drunk patrons
staggering out of the club on your in breath.

❋

Allow several new gas
punters into the club.

Continue this pattern, knowing that you have
quelled the panicked queue of your inward
gasses as well as getting a firm grip on the
basics of nightclub door management.

THE MOSQUITO NET

With this exercise, we celebrate the majesty and beauty of even the smallest of lifeforms. In Bad Owl position, feel the build of inner turbulence. Release a single slow and constant blast as you would with the 'Long Note' exercise, but do this semi-clenched such that the pitch is very high, like a mosquito.

Imagine the mosquito is in the
room moving far and near.

Create the effect of a mosquito
circling towards you by increasing the
force in order to affect volume.

At the loudest high blast, imagine a
mosquito right near your ear.

At the quietest, imagine it is moving away.

Marvel at the tide of life.
The ebb and the flow of us in our efforts
is the same as the mosquito's.

Marvel at how highly pitched you can release
back turbulence when you put your mind to it.

Savour the importance of life on
even the smallest level.

THE MOUTH-GRIPPED KITTEN

This is a reactive exercise in acceptance. It is useful for those times we must endure the excruciation of being shamed or embarrassed by any errant gas we have deposited into the nearby environment.

Should a moment of unwanted
back miasma pass into being,
assume the Bad Owl position.

Relax the neck and arms
such that you are slouched.

Clear your mind and try to tune out
any outside noise (such as the noise
of people complaining angrily about
the sudden dip in air quality).

Your body and mind are now creating
no resistance, in much the same way
that a kitten when lifted by the neck in its
mother's mouth will instinctively relax.

When you feel the glare or pointed finger of those around you, relax the shoulders further and think of kittens. Really nice kittens.

Wait for any drama to subside before coming out the of Mouth-gripped Kitten exercise.

TIP

The acquisition of an actual cat, complete with litter of kittens, is encouraged for this exercise. It is, however, important to remember that a cat is not just for the cementation of mindful flatulence exercises.

THIS TOO MUST PASS

Grouping life experiences with any current flatulence is a glorious occurrence and helps us understand change. Though there is an element of crudity to it, for which I apologize.

Whatever the moment, focus on
it as your flatulence rises.

Be mindful of the moment's fragility in time.

On passing gas, release also the
moment, saying, 'This moment, like
the gas of my ass . . . must pass.'

TIP

This exercise is as effective during a crisis as it is in a moment of jubilation. It also works for averagely disappointing experiences, such as a bad bus journey or a tepid bath.

WIND CHIPOLATAS

This is exactly the same as wind sausages but shorter and more abundant. It is also possible to advance to a smaller size and therefore greater abundance than the chipolata, more like Viennese sausages and known as 'Wind Wieners'. Or, in the right circumstances, approximate the powerfully flavoured Spanish sausage, which is then usually called 'Chorizo Chuffs'.

THE WISHING
SKY LANTERN

Similar to the This Too Must Pass exercise but different in almost every way, the Wishing Sky Lantern concerns us with the future and our wildest dreams.

Braced in the Flying Starfish position, close
your eyes and identify your heart's desire.
Perhaps this is the love of a person, or
something simpler like wanting a better car.

❁

Form the wish and feel its energy rise
like the gasses you are due to emit.
Say loudly 'Flying starfish, carry this
wish, Heavens you owe me this.'

❁

Deploy the leap of the Flying Starfish and
release the wish from your behind along
with the gas (also from your behind).

❁

Imagine the wish floating up to the
Heavens like a floating lantern.
If anyone asks you what you just did, say
'nothing' and they will soon not believe
they saw and heard it anyway.

THE MAGIC CARPET

This exercise lifts our spirits and tests the limits of our imagination. The experience of the exercise could be heightened further by the sourcing of pantaloons, the procurement of a magic lamp and a companion who is prepared to sit with you with their shirt off and pretend to be a genie.*

Find a rug in your house. If you do not have
a rug, then a towel will do. If you do not have
a towel, then buy a towel. Everyone needs
a towel but not everyone needs a rug.

Sit on the rug in sitting Shattered Puffin
position. Imagine yourself to be on a
magic carpet, perhaps bought from a
tinker in an old market square.

Close your eyes and ready yourself
to emit one blast of flatus.

On emitting the blast, feel the rug or
pretend towel rug fly up into the air.

Imagine the rug lowering slowly
as you do emit gas.

As you next emit gas, imagine
the rug soaring up again.

Feel calm as you look down on the kingdom below
and feel proud that you are self-powering your
own magic carpet with your own gas which is
good for the environment in more ways than one.

*Quiet Paul was at first reluctant to assist with this exercise
before I reminded him that he had at that stage slipped
behind with repayments for the glass coffee table he had
rendered unusable after his careless accident. As a result,
Quiet Paul became an eager genie for my ride even offering
to paint himself blue for the purpose.

THE LIGHTNING'S THUNDER: A FARTING FABLE

Once there was a hungry Lightning that would flash in the sky during storms and strike steeples and weather vanes, eating them up and leaving them charred. The Lightning consumed everything it could. It was reckless and even cruel.

It would consume the sheep on the top of the hill one after another, burning their wool. It would electrocute the top of shepherds' crooks, causing the shepherds to need time off work.

The Lightning could not be stopped. With each surge of power, it ate up the land with no sign of stopping.

One day, the god Jupiter saw the Lightning eating up the side of a sheepy hill. It bellowed, 'Lightning! I know you must eat land and sheep but you have been greedy. From now on, you will know what it is to have to process humbly and to digest.'

And with that, Jupiter bestowed intestines on the lightning. From then on, after everything the Lightning ate, be it grass, sheep or shepherd, it would need to wait, digest and then fart out that which it had consumed. Each fart would rattle round the heavens and could be heard by all.

From then on, the Lightning struck only when it needed to and farted out thunder one, two, three, four or five seconds later, depending on the size of its hill meal.

The moral to this tale is thus:
That which we sow with our mouths
shall be reaped by our bottoms.

MINDFUL FLATULENCE MANTRAS

In the course of following the daily path of our lives, we will be dealt different scenarios in the same way that our bottoms deal differing gusts of flatulent air. There are many mantras available to us for these varied situations and these gas affirmations can be used presumptively or reactively. It is good to get into the habit of uttering them when the time for each is right. A mantra is a repeated chant, so it is befitting that there are mantras for our daily eructations, which, let's face it, are and forever will be repeated. The vocal element to each mantra should ideally match the report of the gaseous backdraft in terms of volume.*

---

*Obviously, this is not always possible if you are limited by your surroundings or are in difficult company, or you are Quiet Paul. Quiet Paul's voice is so quiet now that I actively encourage him to communicate via farts. For example, one fart is yes, two farts are no and three farts mean, 'I have finally reimbursed you for the coffee table I fell through and damaged beyond repair.'

OMG

Like the Buddhist mantra 'ohm', this can be used to tune into the surprise that a wind can cause when it exudes from us. Perhaps the report of the flatulence is loud or perhaps it is what lingers thereafter. In such cases 'OMG' (from the abbreviation 'OH MY GAS'!) can be uttered. This steadying mantra can be used at all times. Repeat the mantra ten times for full effect.

'OMG, OMG, OMG, OMG, OMG, OMG, OMG, OMG, OMG, OMG'

GAS YIN AND GAS YANG

Making us mindful of the balance of nature, this simple mantra can soothe us in the aftermath of any of the bigger blasts that we create.

'I was filled full, now I am fulfilled.'

POSITIVE AFFIRMING FART MANTRAS

Often an episode of flatulence can leave us at our most vulnerable, so in these moments it is invaluable to make positive affirmations. They may seem to go against the grain of reality in the moment but it is important to declare them bravely whenever we produce back miasma. On producing a loud utterance from our hindquarters, we must counter with one of the following, even if we are in a public library.

'I radiate confidence and others respect me.'

'I am a decent person who respects community.'

'I am attractive to all of those around me.'

'My confidence grows with
everything I create.'

'I attract new clients to the workplace.'

FART MANTRAS
OF NATURE

An awareness of what one's flatulence is to nature can be a very positive thing. So it is important to use the mantras of nature whenever we relieve ourselves gaseously outdoors.

'To the trees my wind is a song.'

'A breeze will always go in the
direction it wishes to go.'

'The skies have an extra cloud
tonight. And they are grateful.'

**'Let the tides of the sea be
moved by mighty wind.'**

FART WHISPERING MANTRAS

A big part of mindful flatulence is respect. We must have respect for our bottom air. We must listen to it as well as talk to it. Fart whispering is a great way to pass on this common respect for our hindquarter nonsenses. We must talk to them like they are a person.

'Go well, the ghost of my backside.'

'You are the sky and everything
else is weather.'

'Like broken fish repaired in me
– I to the ocean set you free.'

GUST LISTENING MANTRAS

The Gust Listening Mantras practised by the Oink Vicars of Eritrea are unique in that they are not spoken. Instead they are imagined. Moreover, we must hear them as if they are the words of our own bottom. So, for these mantras, we need peace and silence as we hear our own emissions speak to us, offering us steadying praise.

'You are strong, you are beautiful, you are enough.'

'Thank you for your caring for me, most gracious host.'

'I emerge from the tunnel of your grace and all is well.'

THE ALL PRESENT AND CORRECT FART MANTRAS

At times in our flatulent lives, we risk extracurricular activity which can be uncomfortable and involve a great deal of underwear administration. To this end, it is important to be thankful for the times when this doesn't occur. The All Present and Correct Mantras help us to affirm this.

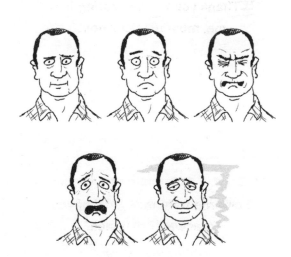

'I feel safe and
comfortable in my body.'

'I am grateful to the universe that
this has gone well.'

'Grant me the strength to stop any
extracurricular activity that I can, the
patience to accept the extracurricular
activity I cannot, and the wisdom to
know the difference.'

THE NOT SO PRESENT AND CORRECT FART MANTRAS

At those times when we fall to the menace of backwater whilst emitting back wind it is important to acknowledge it with this simple mantra, especially if other people are present.

'I learn from my mistakes.'

FLATULENT SOCIAL EMOTIONS AND THEIR MANTRAS

Emotions experienced upon emitting wind in company are as varied as the many flatulences themselves. It is important to be able to identify each one in order to know which the correct mantra is to be announced prior to deployment of the flatulence.

PRIDE

More often than not, flatulence is the bringer of confidence in oneself. Sometimes it is the dealer of the miasma who may find the experience the most amusing and will endeavour some level of gusto into his or her gust. The Pride mantra varies from place to place but is the most common and the most widely recognized of the Flatulent Social Emotion Mantras. Take up Listing Monk (Proud), Big-eyed Crow or Flying Starfish pose and repeat the Pride mantra, which is thus:

'Listen to this, it's too good to miss, I'm the number one!'

MIRTH

This is an emotion that flatulence can give to others, usually if there's an element of surprise, such as during a science exam or a minute's silence. The mantra goes thusly:

'Yes, it's a fart, gave you a start,
I'm the number one!'

SHAME

Whilst churches of flatulence do not encourage the feeling of shame in relation to any bottom activity, they do acknowledge its existence. The Shame mantra can come before or after a gas, given its nature. It should be broadcast in Listing Monk (Bashful) or Shattered Puffin position and go like this:

'I am to blame, yes I'm ashamed,
I'm not the number one.'

FEAR

Again, this is an emotion that all churches of flatulence frown upon but accept. In the same way you would frown on but accept someone wearing bright turquoise footwear to a funeral. In Big-eyed Crow the mantra should go thus:

'That can't be right. I feel a fright,
take me to hospital (please).'

ABUNDANCE

We all know if a back wind is a lone wolf or just one of a burgeoning hunting pack. On the occasions when we are certain our miasma will be joined by its colleagues, the mantra of Abundance must be announced socially. In any position, the mantra is as follows:

'That was but one, it's not yet gone,
here's comes its brethren now!'

THE GASSY SOW
AND THE COCKEREL:
A FARTING FABLE

Once there was a Gassy Sow who lived on a farm with a Cockerel. The Cockerel's job was to wake everyone first thing in the morning. The Gassy Sow's gas would build up over the day and would escape loudly sometime in the middle of the night at such a volatile rate it would make her teats wobble. This caused the Gassy Sow great shame. She was mocked by the cruel Cockerel.

'Look at you with your stomach all filled with gas,' the Cockerel would say. 'Don't you wish you were like me? Light and free and on a diet of grain?'

The poor sow would sob herself to sleep, weighed down by the shame and unhappy with her body image, given the influences of porcine fashion at that time.

One day, the farmer saw the Gassy Sow oinking sadly and bloating up for her one big emission that would come later that night. He put her on diet of grain also to ease the gasses within her. For the first time in many years, the Gassy Sow slept soundly and without discomfort or shame.

When she woke, the farm was in chaos. The cattle were lowing un-milked in the sheds, the sheep were bleating unshorn and the cockerel remained sound asleep in a bucket.

The farmer rushed in and shot the Cockerel for failing to wake the farm. As the Cockerel croaked its last few breaths it lamented, 'Oh Gassy Sow. It was your single loud night fart that always woke me such that I could wake the farm – I have mocked you wrongly for your parping had purpose.'

The Cockerel was replaced by another cockerel that was much more 'woke' and the sow went back to being gassy and was never mocked at that farm ever again.

The moral of the story is thus: One man's shame is another's alarm clock.

YOUR MINDFUL
FLATULENCE JOURNAL

During my Year of Discovery, I was compelled to make notes of my journey. I found that the days on which I achieved Supreme Gas were the days where I remained focused on my fart donkeys (see page 53).

We often forget to remain present during moments of miasma. It's crucial that we all remember to stay in the present and learn how to release our minds and our bottoms as one. It can be useful to keep a note of moments where your body has trumped and triumphed together, so you can remind yourself on more difficult days when your wind doesn't pass through your back passage with pleasant relief.

Sometimes we can feel out of balance, and I hope in these pages you can make notes on where you have been going wrong. As I tell all of my students, feeling truly zen is only a fart away, if you just allow it. So, pick up a pen and start venting your thoughts as you release.

STAY IN THE MOMENT

Make a note of how you are feeling. Have you released? And if not, when do you plan to release? Take a moment to think about your gas and where you want it to escape. Also, take some time to think about how you react with other's miasmas. Are you appreciative or do you run for the hills with your hand over your mouth? Changing your attitude comes from deep within, beyond the bowels.

I plan to release my gas . . .

When I release my gas, I will feel . . .

~~~~~~~~~~~~~~~~~~~~~~~~~~

~~~~~~~~~~~~~~~~~~~~~~~~~~

~~~~~~~~~~~~~~~~~~~~~~~~~~

When others release their gas, I feel . . .

~~~~~~~~~~~~~~~~~~~~~~~~~~

~~~~~~~~~~~~~~~~~~~~~~~~~~

~~~~~~~~~~~~~~~~~~~~~~~~~~

Lastly, what does it smell like? Immerse yourself in the gasses, wherever they have come from; they were intended for you.

~~~~~~~~~~~~~~~~~~~~~~~~~~

~~~~~~~~~~~~~~~~~~~~~~~~~~

MINDFUL FLATULENCE IS . . .

What does Mindful Flatulence mean to you? Write down the first thoughts that come to mind and what the practise can do for you. Be free when you scribble down your thoughts, there is no judgement here.* Are there any negative thoughts swirling in your mind and in your bowels? Dispel them here once and for all.

What is mindful flatulence to you?

*Apart from Quiet Paul. He doesn't make much noise, but he can give you a stinker of a glare if he's not happy with you.

PLAN TO BE PRESENT

For some of us, becoming mindfully flatulent is as natural as fake tan. And by that, I mean, full of patches and with strange gaps around the ankles. It's important that you make a list of your goals for the day, the week and the month. What do you want to achieve with your gasses?

It's important to find what works for you. I am not an evening person, so I find it best to rise before dawn and squeeze out at least a dozen zephyrs before breakfast. If you plan properly, you will be able to access the dark patches in your flatulent journey so far, and get scrubbing on them, if you know what I mean. When do you feel most at ease with your farts? Plan to release as mindfully as you can at the same time every day.

I fart best . . .

**I was taken by surprise
when I farted ...***

*The farts that take us by surprise are filled with much more joy than the ones we plan. The secret to success is to make every fart feel like a surprise to yourself and others around you, even if it's been scheduled. The endorphins you release from a surprised face are just as important as the fart itself.

YOUR FLATULENCE LOG

You may think for a moment that I have progressed from flatulence to full bowel release, but no, I merely mean that it's imperative to keep a note of your memorable zephyrs – big and small. We can often forget the sweet happiness of a release and it's important that you celebrate each one as a success.

MY TOP FIVE
TRUMPS

1.

2.

3.

4.

5.

Why they made the top five

**What I can do in future farts
to make them a top five**

THE COLOUR OF JOY

When your fart escapes into the world, do you imagine what colour it is? I think of mine as releasing in intermittent colours of the rainbow, but that's only because I had an unpleasant reaction to a vodka and soda in 2006 and I can only see in technicolour when in miasma. Are your farts a deep blue, as deep as the ocean, swirling around your flatulent receivers with the same dark intent as the tide? Or are they pink fluffy clouds, as light as candyfloss and filled with an inexplicable amount of e-numbers?

Imagine your farts now and colour them in.

THE GRATITUDE OF FARTS

In order to progress to the level of Gas Cleric, you must allow gratitude to escape your bowels every time. Just as we repeat the mantras during each exercise, we must allow ourselves to fully acknowledge the incredible ability of our bodies to produce such an astonishing mix of sound and smell.

Write down ten different feelings that farting has given you. It's okay to mix feelings together, like the time when I did a miasma so strong in the local library, that I was filled with mirth and deep pride all at once.

1.

2.

3.

4.

5.

6.

7.

8.

9.

10

STAY WITH THE WIND

A BRIEF NOTE ON HOW TO MAINTAIN MINDFUL FLATULENCE IN YOUR EVERYDAY LIFE

And so your passage with me is concluded and you are set free into the world, wiser, fuller and with much more to give off to the universe. I am saddened that our time together has passed, just like a flighty zoom of gas must pass from our inner cavities into the outside world, or a truck must sometimes pass a house.

I urge you to keep this small tome in your back pocket where possible, such that you can absorb its reading and then bestow it upon another trainee flatulantee. Though my publisher is not crazy about this idea and will not expand on why.

For any of you who fear the valuable teachings from this book will fade from your memory as quickly as a fat man in a heatwave, I leave you with a final affirmation. Flatulence is all around us and, just as a bird will fly to the heavens, so too will your fart. That fart will be like a mini alarm, a reminder to you that you absorbed all the teachings of mindful flatulence and that you must hold them close to you at all times.

That fart will remind you that you have the exercises and spiritual writings from the Magna Farta in your hands. You can put that fart on snooze but it will be back as another reminding fart. There will always be a fart to remind you to stay flatulently mindful. To stay mindful of farting and of farts.

I apologize for using the word fart so much in this closing section. Within this book, I have used many more kindly terms for fart as you will have realized, but I now understand from my editor that I have not hit the quota for using the actual word 'fart'.

Therefore, I fart hope you will forgive me for fart using the word fart excessively in these fart final fart fart stages. Fart.

Sail off now my firm friend, like a magnificent ship, with the wise wind forever at your back. Go well.

Gus T. Blooms